CW00665502

why I loved you

IRIS SONG

Copyright © 2022 Iris Song
All rights reserved. This book or any portion thereof
may not be reproduced or used in any manner
whatsoever without the express written permission of
the author except for the use of brief quotations in a
book review or on social media.

for the ones
still healing
from lost love
and broken hearts

Loss

why I loved you by iris song

this is the tragedy of it:
i have walked through
a thousand rooms
and met a thousand people
but not one of them
could make my heart beat
the same way you do,
each beat in my chest
is a reminder

-    *why i loved you*

i come from the kind of place
where safety is a luxury
not a right

the kind of place
where it is normal
for someone to be crying at night

i guess that is why
i mistook you for safety
when you were a tragedy

waiting
to happen
to me

why I loved you by iris song

they talk about storms
with human names
but if they met you
they would ask why
wildfires aren't named
after people too

storms leave something
behind in their wake
wildfires leave nothing
but ashes and smoke

all this time i mistook your warmth
for love when you were the fire
that was destroying me

     -   *like a moth to a flame*

why I loved you by iris song

it was the way you looked
at me across the room
how you said my name
like it was a secret
your voice low and slow
a crooked smile across your face

-   *i knew you were trouble the minute i saw you.*

i wish we had begun as friends. i wish i had learned about you slowly, with all the time in the world. where the conversations at midnight began with laughter, silliness and not an enduring hope it was more. i wish love had come to us in gentle waves instead of an ocean storm. i think it would have been better that way knowing all your flaws and your good parts without feeling like we were in a hurry to get somewhere. i have learned since knowing you that people are not a destination but a journey. i wish we had begun as friends because i would have learned that i should not trust my heart with you as a lover. and perhaps that way we would still be in each others lives, still know each other.

i promised myself that this time i will tell no one, that the kindling in my chest would burn down a thousand bridges, so i kept it all to myself, i let it weigh me down, i carried it all on my own back and sometimes i wonder how much lighter i would feel today if i had taken a match and lit everything up, watched the beauty of the flames as i burned it all down.

i can't tell my friends we didn't work out.
not after i have obsessed over your eyes
and your smile and the scar over your eyebrow.
they warned me about you and i loved you anyway.
i can't bear the shame of having to admit
they were right about you

i know there are no trophies for this:
but i tried with all my heart
to love you the way you needed me to.

   -   *i just wish it was enough*

love is supposed to be
the most tender thing
that ever happened to you.
it's supposed to be
cotton candy soft,
a warm gentle blanket
to wrap around yourself
on a cold, cold day.
it shouldn't make you feel
like you are shut out in the dark
trying your best
to make it home.

- *lessons i learned after you left 1*

when i was five years old
i was convinced flying
was something humans
could do easily,
that in the air we would sprout
invisible wings
so i climbed to the top of the stairs
and leapt...

the result was a broken leg
and a broken wrist
that never quite healed right

the doctor said
i was lucky to escape
with my life

what i'm trying to say is:

you are more dangerous
than the most dangerous thing
i ever did to myself.

why I loved you by iris song

i never thought
i would have to live in a world
where we do not know each other
anymore
where i must mourn you
while you are still alive

-    *no one taught me how to grieve the living*

why I loved you by iris song

its humiliating to think
how badly i wanted
to beg you to stay.

   -    *when you didn't want me at all*

you made me feel whole again
just to smash me
into a million
pieces.

- *the heart doesn't break it shatters*

why I loved you by iris song

they told me that alcohol
would eventually numb the pain,
but something about the bitterness
at the end of every drink
reminds me of you

   -    *you are the last push i needed to get sober*

why I loved you by iris song

i am the kind of broken
where i can no longer
feel the suns warmth
or see its light ever again

the worst part of still loving you
in this deep, all consuming, destructive way
is that i do not know
if you ever loved me back

i spend every single moment thinking of you
knowing somewhere inside my soul
not only that you are happy without me
but that you are not even thinking about me

    -    *did you ever really care about me at all?*

why I loved you by iris song

the hardest thing
i have ever had to do
is pretend i don't care
while i watch you fall in love
with someone else

i used to have so much potential,
such a spark and joy for life
until i wasted it all loving you
and getting nothing in return

-   *i miss who i used to be*

WHAT SHOULD I DO WITH ALL THE RAGE
YOU LEFT INSIDE ME. WHAT SHOULD I DO
WITH ALL THE RAGE YOU LEFT INSIDE ME.
WHAT SHOULD I DO WITH ALL THE RAGE
YOU LEFT INSIDE ME. WHAT SHOULD I DO
WITH ALL THE RAGE YOU LEFT INSIDE ME.
WHAT SHOULD I DO WITH ALL THE RAGE
YOU LEFT INSIDE ME. WHAT SHOULD I DO
WITH ALL THE RAGE YOU LEFT INSIDE ME.
WHAT SHOULD I DO WITH ALL THE RAGE
YOU LEFT INSIDE ME. WHAT SHOULD I DO
WITH ALL THE RAGE YOU LEFT INSIDE ME.
WHAT SHOULD I DO WITH ALL THE RAGE
YOU LEFT INSIDE ME. WHAT SHOULD I DO
WITH ALL THE RAGE YOU LEFT INSIDE ME.
WHAT SHOULD I DO WITH ALL THE RAGE
YOU LEFT INSIDE ME. WHAT SHOULD I DO
WITH ALL THE RAGE YOU LEFT INSIDE ME.
WHAT SHOULD I DO WITH ALL THE RAGE
YOU LEFT INSIDE ME. WHAT SHOULD I DO
WITH ALL THE RAGE YOU LEFT INSIDE ME.
WHAT SHOULD I DO WITH ALL THE RAGE
YOU LEFT INSIDE ME. WHAT SHOULD I DO
WITH ALL THE RAGE YOU LEFT INSIDE ME.
WHAT SHOULD I DO WITH ALL THE RAGE
YOU LEFT INSIDE ME. WHAT SHOULD I DO
WITH ALL THE RAGE YOU LEFT INSIDE ME.
WHAT SHOULD I DO WITH ALL THE RAGE
YOU LEFT INSIDE ME. WHAT SHOULD I DO
WITH ALL THE RAGE YOU LEFT INSIDE ME.

my biggest fear about this heartache is that it will never
end, that i will miss you forever and ever,
this bitterness will consume and i will be left alone to
wonder forever if you were supposed to be a chapter, or
an entire book – whether you were it, my great love,
and we ended much too soon.

- *i wish i was afraid of the dark instead*

i'm so afraid i won't know how to heal from this
i'm so scared that this pain is endless
that it will never stop

-   *the sun keeps setting and i never start healing*

i wonder what
i could have done
with all this time
i have spent
worrying
instead.

- *lessons of anxiety*

you don't get to come back just like that.
i am not a hospital for you to come to
when you need someone to love you through pain
only to leave when you feel better
after ignoring that i have needs too.
if you cannot hold me
with the same love i hold you,
i do not want you.

- *boomerang*

you said,
i never meant to hurt you

i told you,
whether you meant to or not,
you did

you said,
i'm sorry.

i asked you,
do you love me enough to fix this?

and you said nothing.

-    *silence is an answer too*

i fell in love with a version of you that never existed and that's on me.

you used the love i had for you to manipulate me and that's on you.

- *i can live with what i did, can you?*

why I loved you by iris song

i hope you weren't the best thing to happen to me
i hope things get better one day
and i don't always miss you
and look for you in every crowd

- *when does the pain end?*

the thing is,
we connected,
it was like
the sun in you
reflected rays off
the moon in me
you made me laugh
like i have never laughed before
it was so easy to be with you
so simple to love you
you fit into my life so easily
you with your sunny smile
that lit up the sky
it's hard to believe
that feeling is gone
because you are gone,
you were the first
and last place
that ever felt like
a home.

why I loved you by iris song

sometimes you fall in love
with a dream
you built inside your head
and not the person
you are giving
all of your love to.

\-   *lessons i learned after you left 2*

why I loved you by iris song

i wish i could stop thinking about you,
your laugh, your smile,
the way you kissed me.

i wish i could stop thinking
about all the good days
because they were so few
and far between.

but the mind is a tricky thing,
it only wants to focus on the good parts.
i know you were bad for me,
but how do i convince my heart?

- *rose tinted glasses.*

why I loved you by iris song

if i could collect the tears
i have cried over you
i would have enough salt water
to fill an ocean

why I loved you by iris song

when people ask me about you
i tell them how much kinder
and gentler and full of love i used to be
until i met you.

    -   *you turned a sun into a ruined star*

if a daughter grows up
constantly seeking
and pleading with her father
for love,

she learns
that she does not deserve
easy, kind love,

but a love that only takes
and never gives anything
in return

- *a father doesn't need to be absent to be absent*

i wish my mother was the kind of mother i could talk to. you know, that *best friend* kind of mother, the *laughs with you all the time* kind of mother, the *sit at the kitchen table and drink hot chocolate with* kind of mother, the *tell all your problems to and she will always listen to you* kind of mother.

maybe if i had a mother like that, i could tell her all about you and how you broke my heart. but my mother and i don't talk. not like that.

- *when mother asks me how my day was, i just say fine*

why I loved you by iris song

i am so scared i will forget
the music in your voice
when you said my name

it felt like you were the sun to my earth,
but really you were simply a rogue star
that invaded this solar system
and then turned into a black hole
that destroyed everything
in its wake

the theory says that
there are an infinite number of universes
and in those infinite number of universes
there are an infinite number of ways
we could have met and fallen apart
and i'd like to think
that in at least some of them
you love me back the way
i needed you to in this one
and we practice a *forever*
instead of a *maybe*

i stopped going to therapy
because i could say nothing
i don't know how to explain
the magnitude of what you did to me
to a stranger

- *i can't even begin to explain it to myself*

why I loved you by iris song

i sometimes wonder
why losing you hurts this much
when loving you
was so deeply exhausting,
i felt tired all the way
to my bones
every single day
when loving you.
some days i am relieved
you are gone
but on others i miss you
because god, at least
i felt *something*
now i fell nothing
at all.

-   *the relief and discomfort of feeling nothing*

there is a theory that says
that the flapping of a butterfly's wings
can lead to a hurricane halfway across the world

you were the butterfly
to my hurricane,
the chaos to my peace

i am building myself a chrysalis
to hide in and become a better version of me
the kind of person who can forget

why i *ever* loved you.

Healing

why I loved you by iris song

last night,
the moon told me a secret
she said

i have watched a thousand lifetimes
of lovers fall in and out of love
with each other and leave

but i have yet to see someone
learn to love themselves
and then leave

-   *moon song*

why I loved you by iris song

stop looking for safety
in the same place
where danger knows your name

    -   *you will never heal where you broke*

why I loved you by iris song

remember how like the rain
you are always enough to nourish
what wants to grows

but you will never be enough
for what does not want to grow

-    *its not you its them*

you are destined for better love than this
a *never leave you* kind of love
a *love you through the bad times* kind of love
a *sunshine or rain* kind of love
an *i'll be the dark to your sun* kind of love
a *lets fight our demons together* kind of love
the love you deserve will find you.

-   *a promise*

it's all right to want love, and hope it finds you. it's okay to wish a good love for yourself one day. but in the meantime, seek that love within your own heart. learn how to love every piece of yourself, all those same pieces you wish someone else would love.

i'm sorry no one ever told you this
but living will hurt.
it will bruise you when you least expect it
and break you when you hope it doesn't.
living is not for the faint hearted,
and there is no one,
not one person among us
who makes it out of this alive.
but you will love and be loved
more than you will hurt.
you will break but you will heal.
and the version of yourself
that you become will be better,
braver, more beautiful every time.
stay. stay to watch the chrysalis open.
stay to watch yourself become
the butterfly.

bruce lee once said that to get through life, we should be like water, ever adapting to whatever situation we are put in. my mother says, when life gives you lemons, bake yourself a cake. both these analogies involve taking what happened to you and turning it into something easier to bear. i try to think of this broken heart the same way. carefully i piece each shattered piece back into the shape it once was, pour gold through the cracks.

you think i won't recover from what you did to me? i'll wear my scarred heart like a prize. look, look how its scars glow in the sun.

- *kintsugi*

why I loved you by iris song

i guess my heart still feels
like we have unfinished business
like there is a story between us
that was never written,
an ending that was more
than a haunting silence.

- *i just want closure*

why I loved you by iris song

you have never been too much
you have just been seeking love
in the arms of people
who are not ready
for the beautiful way you shine

- *you light up every room you walk into*

you do not have to change for anyone's love. the right person will never make you feel less than in any way. you deserve the kind of love that doesn't demand a better, prettier, more accomplished version of you. you deserve the kind of love that makes you feel like you are enough because you are. just like this. *you are enough.*

i am sorry no one protected you when you needed it the most. you have always been the brightest, shining thing about me. when things get bad, you have made me laugh. when hope is nowhere to be found, you find something to be hopeful for. you try to cheer me up when i'm at my saddest, and have never abandoned me like so many others have and still, i have not appreciated you. i am sorry it has taken me so long to learn how to protect you. but i will be everything you needed when you needed love the most. you will never have to be afraid or feel small again. i promise.

-   *for my inner child*

i understand now
that we are better apart
than we ever were together
that sunflowers must grow
in a different way than roses,
but it still hurts when i listen
to a song and it reminds me
so much of how you were once
my favourite person in the world

- *sunflowers and roses*

why I loved you by iris song

in another lifetime,
we are kind to each other
we meet at the right time
i tell you that i love you
you smile and say forever
and we go out to watch the sunset.

-   *in a place we do not end*

maybe i was the one
who ruined it for us in the end

maybe i am so difficult
to love that you couldn't stay

maybe i am just
unlovable

- *my worst fears*

*why **I** loved you* by iris song

maybe i'm so angry
all of the time
because everyone
keeps saying
that i should
move on
when you took
everything that
mattered
to me with you

-    *what i should have said in therapy 1*

people try to convince you that healing is a mountain, and it isn't. healing is a country where you must fight forest fires, battle through a hundred hurricanes, think you have got to the other side and do it all over again until you run out of fires and hurricanes.

you may never be fully recovered, but you will always get up and fight again.

- *why survivor rhymes with warrior*

i'm trying to be okay with the fact that i can never talk to my parents the way other people can talk to theirs. i am trying to accept the distance between us and not constantly hope for them to say *i am so proud of you.*

-     *i am whole with or without their love*

the thing is,
i fell hard.

i fell hard
and you didn't.

and in a universe
of infinite possibilities,

there was always a chance
you could fall with me.

but you didn't

-   *it doesn't stop me wishing you had*

sometimes your soulmate meets you at the wrong time. sometimes your soulmate turns out to be an unkind person. sometimes your soulmate breaks your heart and leaves you shattered.

no one ever tells you that sometimes it goes wrong with your soulmate and you are left holding your own broken soul.

-   *the truth about soulmates*

why I loved you by iris song

i'm no longer sure
what hurts more

is it better to be someone's option
or not to be loved by them at all?

what to do after your heart breaks

breathe. drink water. eat a lot of ice cream. cry until you
are too tired to cry anymore. watch a sad movie so you
can truly get every tear out. then watch something
happy instead. call a friend over so you aren't alone. put
your phone away so you stop looking at their photos on
social media. find a song that does not remind you of
them and play it on repeat. get angry, really angry.
scream into a pillow. scream into the wind. take your
dog for a walk, if you don't have a dog, go walking
alone. eat more ice cream. cry some more. make sure
you do not cry yourself to sleep. make it your ritual to
text your friends good night instead of him. make an
anti love playlist. play it on repeat. whatever you do, do
not cry yourself to sleep. breathe. just breathe.

when the haze of love finally lifted,
i understood that you saw me as a means to an end
that you saw yourself as fire to my kindling
a distraction rather than a real love,
you saw me as a pit stop,
a hotel room to rest your bones
rather than a home
full of love and laughter and joy

in the grand scheme of things,
i am glad we happened,
despite all the pain,
but no, you do not get to leave
and also have me in your life,
you see it may suit you
to not be with me
but also have me around
but it will break me to see you
with somebody else

-     *no, we can't still be friends*

i have always loved full heartedly.
no one taught me how to love in half measures,
weigh out love on a measuring scale
and give out just enough
you either have all of my heart
or you have none of it.

- *what it's like to love an ocean*

you can't fix people you can only fix yourself.
you can't fix people you can only fix yourself.
you can't fix people you can only fix yourself.
you can't fix people you can only fix yourself.
you can't fix people you can only fix yourself.
you can't fix people you can only fix yourself.
you can't fix people you can only fix yourself.
you can't fix people you can only fix yourself.
you can't fix people you can only fix yourself.
you can't fix people you can only fix yourself.
you can't fix people you can only fix yourself.
you can't fix people you can only fix yourself.
you can't fix people you can only fix yourself.
you can't fix people you can only fix yourself.
you can't fix people you can only fix yourself.
you can't fix people you can only fix yourself.
you can't fix people you can only fix yourself.
you can't fix people you can only fix yourself.
you can't fix people you can only fix yourself.
you can't fix people you can only fix yourself.
you can't fix people you can only fix yourself.
you can't fix people you can only fix yourself.
you can't fix people you can only fix yourself.
you can't fix people you can only fix yourself.
you can't fix people you can only fix yourself.
you can't fix people you can only fix yourself.
you can't fix people you can only fix yourself.
you can't fix people you can only fix yourself.
you can't fix people you can only fix yourself.
you can't fix people you can only fix yourself.
you can't fix people you can only fix yourself.
you can't fix people you can only fix yourself.

people either grow to meet you
and then you grow together
or they stay exactly where they are
and expect you to meet them
as far as they have met
themselves

-   *things i learned in therapy 2*

if i look back in honesty, i don't think we were ever good for each other. and for the longest time, i blamed myself thinking if i just did enough to make you happy, we could keep being together. i justified your cruelty because i thought i deserved it, and you justified my sadness thinking some people are simply born sad. i was so desperate to make this work, that i was willing to look past everything we did to each other just so you stayed and i did not have to be alone again.

-   *things i learned in therapy 3*

it took me a long time to understand this
but sometimes we fall in love with people
who we understand will wreck our hearts
because there is more safety
in the destruction you know
than the destruction
you cannot see coming

-   *looking for trouble*

i will forever be in mourning for the person i was before you destroyed me. but i have learned to burn that version of myself, i even sang at her funeral, when i rose from her ashes, i promised her i will be a person she is proud of instead of a person who was so desperate to be loved by you.

-   *phoenix rising*

i like myself better
this way
not in love
but learning
how to love
a person who is worthy
and that person
has my own name

you know how they say, 'if he wanted to, he would'? i
think about that all the time. you see the way you acted
towards me boils down to three things

1. you cared but you didn't care enough to know
   you were hurting me, despite me telling you
2. you knew you were hurting me and you
   understood what you were doing, but you were
   enjoying my pain too much to stop
3. you knew you were hurting me, you understood
   what you were doing but you just couldn't bring
   yourself to try hard enough to stop, which
   means i just wasn't worth it

i have tried to understand what this means time and
time again. and each time, it comes down to this: if he
wanted to love you truly, he would stop hurting you.
but he didn't. so he wouldn't.

how do you picture yourself when you daydream?
do you see yourself as thinner?
do you see yourself prettier?
do you really believe making yourself different
will make you more lovable than you already are?

do you not know
that you deserve love right here,
right now, exactly as you are?

-   *the real version of you is enough*

prioritise your happiness
prioritise your well being
prioritise all the things that bring you joy
prioritise yourself the way you would
prioritise the person you fall in love with

one day people will know me
and they will know the version of me
that is no longer in love with you
a version of me that no longer
speaks of you like you
built the sun
a version of me
that no longer
says your name
like it is magic

more than anything, i hope i am brave enough to risk my heart being broken again. i hope i love this deeply, this openly again. my grandfather on his deathbed told me, *'do not weep for me, for i have loved and been loved. what more could i ask for from life?* and its true. for what more is there to life than to love, love wholeheartedly and perhaps, maybe if we are very lucky, be loved as much in return.

-    *i still believe in love even though it broke me.*

i'd like to think that
somewhere in another universe
you walk into a museum
and stand next to me
as we both admire
the same painting.
when i turn to you and smile,
you smile back and say
"hello."

- *maybe there is a version of us that makes it*

Love Again

i was always afraid
i could never love again,
not after my heart was shattered
so cruelly and the pain left welts
across my soul,
who would want me this way?
i told myself,
all broken and in pieces.

then you came along
with your gentle disposition
and your way of making me laugh
and helped me believe again.

- *second chances*

all i ever wanted was to feel safe
someone to stroke my hair
and tell me everything would be okay
in the worst moments
someone who knew
the way i liked my coffee
and held my hand at 2AM
someone who knew how to be the light
in the moments i couldn't find the sun
someone who loved the stars
and the night sky as much as I do

-   *that's why the universe led me to you*

why I loved you by iris song

the best thing about us
is that we don't have to pretend.
i know all your scars
and you know mine.
we aren't trying to save each other
we are just trying to love one another
and that's how to healing happens.
with acceptance and a whole lot of love

-    *this is how we heal*

loving you was like coming home
to a part of myself
i never even knew existed

    -   *you made me believe in myself again*

why I loved you by iris song

i never thought i could ever be happy
until you told me how beautiful i am,
you called me the sun of your solar system
and i wondered how someone like you
could ever love someone like me.
i always saw myself as nothing special
until you happened to me.

of all the universes
that exist,
i never stop thinking
about how blessed this one is
because this is the one
in which we meet.

why I loved you by iris song

when i was young,
i searched for safety
but never ever found it
until your arms
became my favourite hiding place

- *thank you for making my inner child feel safe*

you helped me understand
silence as a love language,
where we could sit for hours
and hours together
and not ever feel bored
or tired of each other
that sometimes words
aren't needed to say
i love you

why I loved you by iris song

i've been telling the night sky
about our love
and how you have turned
every moment into a thing of wonder

-     *the stars told me to take care of you*

it's two am
and the road outside my house
is silent, darkness covers everything
the streetlight flickers,
even the moon is lying low,
afraid to disturb a sleeping world
and yet here we are together
asking each other about magic
about how everything and nothing
came to be just so our love could exist.

- *conversations at 2am*

i used to write poems when i was lonely,
but now i write them for you.

-    *you made me want to write love poems*

all i've ever wanted is someone to say,
i want to get old with you,
i want us to sit on the porch
silver hair, hot cups of tea
and blankets on our laps
i will still look at you
like you are the best thing
that ever happened to me,
even after all of these years pass
you will always be the best thing
that ever happened to me

i've never really wanted too much. i just want a bit of kindness, a heart that is gentle with mine. i want to help someone fight their demons and hope they will help me fight mine. i want a home with someone which is as warm as tea on an autumn day, as cosy as a blanket while watching the rain.

you are the safety
i have looked for my whole life
look at the way your kindness
makes my inner child
come out of hiding and laugh

- *i haven't heard her laugh in years*

why I loved you by iris song

you are always the best part
of the worst kind of days
and the kindest part of
an unkind, bitter world

i want to love you better than this
a little louder than this
i want to trust you with my whole heart
but you see the last time i did that
the person i trusted handed it back
in a million broken pieces to me.

- *i'm trying, i promise*

truthfully,
i've loved a lot of people i shouldn't have.
and i have loved people badly.
and i still remember all of the names
of all of the people i should have stopped loving
for what they did to me.
too many people left me with so much trauma
that i didn't know how to carry it,
what I'm trying to say,
is forgive me for when it spills out of me.
forgive me for when I am spinning out of control.
i have spent so long loving the wrong people
that i have forgotten what good love looks like.
that it looks like this.
it looks like you.

i stopped waiting for love to come knocking on my
door. i stopped looking at my phone for the text that
would never come. i stopped losing sleep hoping you
would call. i stopped hoping that one day you will
realise the error of your ways and finally come back to
me and apologise. i stopped hoping there was a chance
for us because i realised the more i held onto the idea of
you, the less room in my life for anyone else.

and when I finally let you go, i found someone who
could finally love me back the way i have always
deserved to be loved.

you were the first person to tell me,
"i know you're strong enough
to handle all these burdens alone,
but you are still allowed
to say how heavy they are."

- *this is how you helped me put them down*

mathematically everything about us is an impossibility. if you hadn't been exactly where you were and i hadn't been at the same place at the very same time, the likelihood is that we would never have met. and even if we had crossed paths a few days before or a few days after, there are a million chances we would not be together this way because we may have had other lovers, a different path cut out for us by the universe. that we met, and fell in love, and know each other at all, is a quiet triumph of the universe. and because it could happen for us, i believe that it can happen to anyone, and miracles do exist.

i overthink everything
the way you smiled only a little today
and how your hand shook just slightly
when you lifted your coffee to your lips,
and maybe today you didn't say much
and maybe that means you are tired of me
and that you don't love me.
but then you take my hand
when you see that worried look in my eyes
and say,
"i'm not going anywhere.
i will love you through everything.
through all of this."

- *you make me feel like i am enough*

you are not too much, you have just been placing your love at the feet of all the wrong people

being insecure over your looks is a waste of your time, because someone will love every one of those imperfections.

you are not defined by the people who have left you.

give yourself permission to feel as deeply as you need to.

allow love in when it comes knocking.

-    *5 lessons i learned from you*

i love the way you see the whole world,
how to you the stars are not a graveyard but hope,
how the world is full of more good than evil,
your joy is so infectious,
i love who i am when i am with you.

-   *a place of hope*

what you hate about yourself is the thing someone will love about you. that scar you work so hard to hide is lovely to someone, and that way your hair falls that you find so annoying is what someone will find adorable about you, and the belly you think is too big is beautiful to someone.

listen, what i'm trying to tell you is every bit of you is worthy of love, you just need to see yourself through the eyes of someone who loves you.

why I loved you by iris song

its good if you love a boy
with big strong hands
and a deep laugh
and its good if you love a girl
with long legs who loves art
at the end of the day
what matters is
that we all fall in love
with people
who make us smile
and want us to be
the best of who we are

if he comes back, i hope you tell him that some old flames were meant to die out because they did nothing but set fire to everything they were meant to love. it took you years to rebuild yourself from the ashes he left of you. i hope you remember that.

i used to think the words
"we need to talk" were terrifying
until I met you.

you showed me that
"we need to talk"
means 'lets sit and share our problems'

and 'lets figure out a gentle way
where we do not cause each other harm',
and 'lets communicate without

screaming and shouting'
you showed me
how respect works

you are the first person
who heard my side of the story too
and showed me what its like

to be with someone
who truly
values you.

i am so used to looking
in the mirror
and seeing someone i hate
i forget sometimes
that the person i hate
is also the person you love
and is worthy of my respect

- *on reflection*

i want to be in love with someone who knows how to be
vulnerable in front of me, and i want to be with someone
who knows i will love every broken shard inside them,
and i want to be with someone who looks at me like i'm
the most beautiful person they know and i want to be
with someone who feels lucky i am with them every
single day, and i know this sounds like a whole lot to
ask for, but what it comes down to is this: i want to be
enough for someone, just like i know they will be
enough for me.

-   *enough*

they say sunlight
is the cure for most things
but i promise you only moonlight
has ever soothed my broken heart

- *moonsong*

i'd like to think that when we die,
we become a part of the sun
so every time the sun
lights up the sky
our souls light up in ways
they never got to
when we were alive

-   *soul songs*

i am in love with everything about you.
yes, even your wounds.
yes, even those scars
you are too afraid to show me
for fear that I may leave.
you see those parts of you
that you hide so carefully
do not terrify me.
i welcome them.

i want to meet you as deeply
as you have met yourself.

why I loved you by iris song

i am done
loving people
who tell me
i am too much
to love

i will not settle for the kind of love
that wants me in pieces
that claims i shine too brightly
that i must dim my spark
to be worthy of love

   -   *i am enough and so are you*

*why **I** loved you* by iris song

he was the reason for my insomnia
you are the reason i finally
feel safe enough to sleep

- *thank you for showing me what love really looks like*

you make me feel like i am wanted on a planet that has never felt like home. you make me feel like i am loved in ways i never knew i deserved. you made the outcast in me feel like she has someone who loves her, and the lonely that lives inside me leave. i knew something about you was different the first time i saw you. you make me feel like i am whole. like i am enough.

- *and more than anything i don't doubt that this will last*

i once begged a shooting star
for a love which loved me
without condition.
and a year later here you are,
so maybe, just maybe,
sometimes the stars do listen.

- *starsong*

why I loved you by iris song

i am slowly learning
that some loves
are meant to be felt
and then quietly let go
just like a wild bird
that nests in your window
for a little while
they do not belong
to you forever
they visit just for a season
to give you many lessons
and once you have learned
everything you can
they must be released

- *full moon lessons*

one day you will have the kind of love
like the sky loves the moon
whether in pieces or whole
the sky holds her shine
and lets the moon be exactly
what she needs to

-    *lessons from the full moon*

thank you for showing me
that in a cold world
there are still reasons to love
and love is everything
all of the warmth
that you could ever seek.

    -   *this is why i love you*

About the author

Iris Song is a poet who lives inside a forest. She loves misty mornings, steamy cups of tea and the moon. After her last heartbreak, she decided to write this book hoping that it gives solace to those who have had their heart broken too.

Printed in Great Britain
by Amazon

17366623R00075